MAY THE
PAGES THAT
FOLLOW FILL YOU WITH
HOPE AND WONDER.
MAY THEY REPLENISH YOUR
SOUL.

THIS
LITTLE BOOK OF JOY
BELONGS TO

YOUR NAME

The
LITTLE BOOK
of
JOY

The
LITTLE BOOK
of
JOY

An Interactive Journal
for Thoughts, Prayers, and Wishes

✦

Bill Zimmerman
with illustrations by Tom Bloom

HAZELDEN®

(☾ ✧ ✩

Hazelden
Center City, Minnesota 55012-0176

ISBN: 1-56838-041-0

EDITOR'S NOTE
Hazelden offers a variety of information on chemical
dependency and related areas. Our publications do not
necessarily represent Hazelden's programs, nor do they officially
speak for any Twelve Step organization.

1-800-328-9000 (Toll-Free U.S., Canada, and the Virgin Islands)
1-612-257-4010 (Outside the U.S. and Canada)
1-612-257-1331 (24-Hour FAX)

For my wife, my daughter, and my dog
who provide the bedrock in my life,
and to my friend, Joe Duffy,
who encouraged me to pray.

—BILL ZIMMERMAN

*God, I search for a song in me which I can sing
to You. My voice is not strong, but it is from
my heart. I wish to make music
worthy of Your love.*

PREFACE

This is a book of comfort for both you and me which
we can turn to for some peace of mind. I sewed this
book from the threads of my life at a time of personal
sorrow. The way I held on was to begin writing
these prayersongs as a way to reach the God who
had comforted me as a child. I call them *prayersongs*
because I have always wanted to sing—the written
words are my song. There also are *thanksgivings*, or
words thanking God for the good moments I wish to
remember and appreciate.

You will also find *sweet blessings* accompany-
ing the prayersongs. The blessings are the hoped-for
fulfillments of the prayers I sing. They will do you
good, for there are never enough blessings to go
around in life. I offer them to you and hope you will
accept them and share them with those who are dear
to you. Let them become your own messages of sweet
fortune.

Because I hope my book becomes your own private book of comfort and joy, I have left room on each page for you to write your own prayersongs, reflections, or thoughts, as well as your own sweet blessings. There are spaces, too, for you to write your wishes, your hopes, your dreams, and the special truths you have learned in your life. Perhaps there is even a key word or phrase you wish to jot down that captures your day or how you feel. By writing, you will find that kernel of comfort that always resides within you.

I doubt that your own prayers or hopes are so very different from mine. Perhaps that is the value of picking up this little book of comfort—to learn that we each need the same things in our lives. I hope you will use this homely journal like I do—pick it up when you are feeling lost or in need of succor, and when you are happy too. Keep it handy. May it help you carry on in this wonderful, hard life. May this little book bring joy to your life.

Yours Sincerely,

Bill Zimmerman

EVERYTHING IN
LIFE IS SO
DELICATE;

IT IS A MATTER OF
BALANCE.

I AM PRAYING
MY LIFE OUT TO YOU
LIKE A FISHERMAN WHO
SETS HIS LINE,
WHAT WILL
TODAY'S CATCH BE?

REFLECTION

PAUSE :: STEP BACK TO SEE THE VIEW.

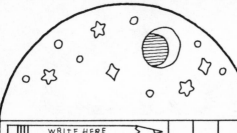

| ▐▐▐ | WRITE HERE ▸ | | D | A | T | E |

☆ SWEET BLESSING ☆

MAY YOU DO AMAZING FEATS.

GoBON

DEAR GOD...
I AM SO THANKFUL
TO BE ALIVE, I THANK YOU
FOR GIVING ME ANOTHER
DAY OF LIFE.
    GRACIAS,

| REFLECTION |

PAUSE... YOU WILL FIND CHUCKLES INSIDE YOU.

| IIII YOUR THOUGHTS | D | A | T | E |

DREAM SPACE

☆ SWEET BLESSING ☆

MAY YOU FIND ONLY BEAUTY
IN THE SOULS OF THE PEOPLE
YOU MEET.

GRACE MEANS
THE FAVOR AND LOVE OF GOD.
AMAZING GRACE TO ME MEANS THE
ABILITY OF GOD TO PARDON US FOR
OUR SINS, OR THE ABILITY WE HAVE
TO FORGIVE OURSELVES. I'D LIKE TO
FORGIVE MYSELF FOR ALL MY FAILURES
AND LIMITATIONS. I'D LIKE TO FIND
FORGIVENESS IN ME.

	REFLECTION	

PAUSE " THE BAD DOESN'T LAST FOREVER.

YOUR SPACE

DATE

☆ SWEET BLESSING ☆

MAY YOU MAKE
WILD FLOWERS AND BERRIES
GROW IN BARREN LAND

GORDON

WHAT
COULD I SAY I ACHIEVED WITH MY LIFE WERE
IT TO END TODAY?
WHAT
MEMORY OF ME WILL LINGER IN THE MINDS OF
THOSE LIVING, AND THOSE WHO WILL COME?
WHAT
WILL MAKE ME SPECIAL?
WHAT
HAVE I DONE WITH MY LIFE TO IMPROVE THE WORLD?
WHAT
DID I DO WITH MY TIME HERE?
WHAT
IS IT TO BE A HUMAN BEING IN THIS WORLD?

	REFLECTION	
	REFLECTION	

PAUSE " YOU CAN JUMP OVER THE HURDLES.

WRITE HERE ⟶ D A T E

A SECRET

☆ SWEET BLESSING ☆

MAY EACH DAY
PROVIDE A NEW BEGINNING FOR YOU.
BE REBORN.

GO ON

WHISPER TO ME,
MY GOD, SO THAT I WILL
BE ALL RIGHT, THAT
ALL WILL GO WELL FOR
THE PEOPLE I LOVE.
AMEN.

REFLECTION
REFLECTION

PAUSE·· THE SUN ALWAYS COMES OUT.

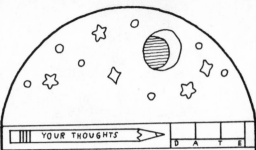

| IIII YOUR THOUGHTS ✏ | | D | A | T | E |

☆ SWEET BLESSING ☆

MAY YOU LEARN
HOW TO WHISTLE.

GO ON

OH, GOD, YOU HAVE MY
LOVE,
YOU HAVE MY
HEART,
CAN YOU NOT THEN SING A
MORE BEAUTIFUL TUNE TO ME?

| REFLECTION |
| REFLECTION |

PAUSE " REMEMBER TO SMILE.

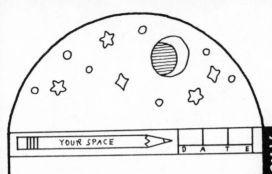

YOUR SPACE		DATE		

☆ SWEET BLESSING ☆

MAY YOU BE STRONG
FOR THE PEOPLE WHO NEED YOU...
AND MOST OF ALL, FOR YOURSELF.

LET
ME
GREET
THE NEW DAY
WITH
HOPE.

REFLECTION

PAUSE " YOU ARE STRONGER THAN YOU THINK.

| ▥ | WRITE HERE → | | D | A | T | E |

☆ SWEET BLESSING ☆

MAY YOU OPEN YOUR HEART
TO LOVE.

GO ON

I GO TO SLEEP NOW,
MY GOD.
BEFORE I SLEEP, I ASK YOUR
BLESSING,
PLEASE WATCH OVER ME.
AMEN.

REFLECTION

PAUSE " TAKE A LEAP OF FAITH.

| ▐▐▐ YOUR THOUGHTS | D | A | T | E |

☆ SWEET BLESSING ☆

MAY YOUR DREAMS
BE SWEET
WHEN YOU SLEEP,

GO ON

DEAR LORD,

PLEASE PROTECT MY FAMILY. PLEASE GRANT THEM GOOD HEALTH AND SOME LAUGHTER, AND THE STRENGTH TO GET THROUGH LIFE'S TOUGH TIMES. GRANT THEM PEACE OF MIND WHEN TIMES ARE BAD. PROTECT THEM WHEN I AM NOT THERE FOR THEM.   AMEN.

REFLECTION

PAUSE " LOOK FOR THE LIGHT.

YOUR SPACE

DATE

BIRTHDAY WISH

☆ SWEET BLESSING ☆

MAY YOU BE BRAVE
ENOUGH TO JUMP THROUGH
FIRE INTO A NEW LAND.

GO ON

WHEN I PRAY TO YOU,
GOD,
I THINK I AM
ALSO FINDING LOVE
IN MY HEART
FOR ME.

| REFLECTION |

PAUSE " BLOW SOME SOAP BUBBLES.

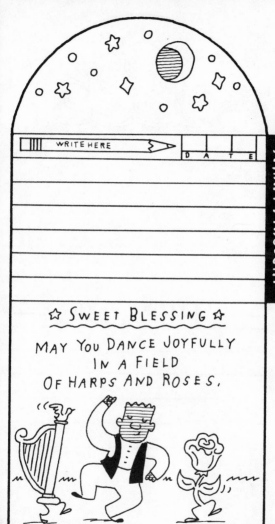

WRITE HERE

DATE

A HAPPY THOUGHT

☆ SWEET BLESSING ☆

MAY YOU DANCE JOYFULLY
IN A FIELD
OF HARPS AND ROSES.

GORDON

YOUR PSALM

| REFLECTION |
REFLECTION

PAUSE

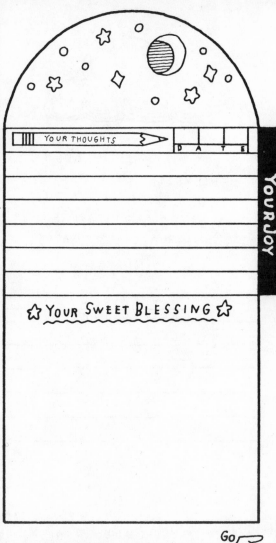

	YOUR THOUGHTS		D	A	T	E

☆ YOUR SWEET BLESSING ☆

YOUR JOY

GO ON

LET ME WALK THROUGH
THE VALLEY OF YOUR DAY,
MY GOD, WITH THE SENSE OF
WONDER AND PLEASURE
THAT RESIDES IN MY NATURE,
TOO.

REFLECTION

PAUSE " PACK YOUR DOUBTS AWAY.

YOUR SPACE | D A T E

SPRING WISH

☆ SWEET BLESSING ☆

MAY YOU FIND
YOUR GREEN PASTURES.

GO
ON

DEAR GOD,

HELP ME BE OPEN
TO YOUR LOVE,

REFLECTION

PAUSE · DANCE WITH YOUR IMAGINATION.

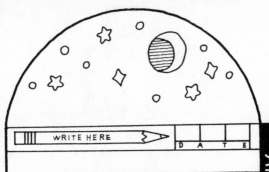

WRITE HERE

DATE

☆ SWEET BLESSING ☆

MAY YOU BATHE IN THE SUN'S RAYS.

WHAT DO YOU HOLD INVIOLATE IN LIFE?
WHAT DO YOU WANT FROM YOURSELF?
WHAT ARE YOU PREPARED TO GIVE?

WHAT IS BEAUTIFUL TO YOU?
WHAT MAKES YOUR MIND SING?
WHEN YOU LOOK, DO YOU FIND GOOD IN YOU?

WHAT IS THE BLESSING YOU WOULD GIVE
   TO THE PEOPLE YOU LOVE?
WHAT TRUTH DO YOU FIND IN YOUR SOUL?
HOW CAN YOU BECOME THE WAY YOU WANT TO BE?

	REFLECTION	

PAUSE ·· BE KIND TO YOURSELF.

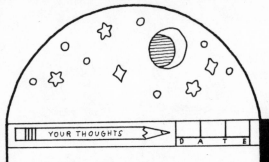

ADVICE

YOUR THOUGHTS

D A T E

☆ SWEET BLESSING ☆

MAY YOU LIVE TO HOLD
RAINBOWS IN YOUR HANDS.

GO ON

OH, GOD,
LET ME FIND THE JOY
IN THE MOMENT
AND HAVE ENOUGH INTELLIGENCE
TO RESPOND
WHEN I ENCOUNTER IT,

REFLECTION

PAUSE " FIND A FLOWER TO SMELL.

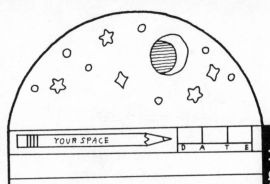

| YOUR SPACE ➡ | D | A | T | E |

☆ SWEET BLESSING ☆

MAY YOU NEVER BE AT A LOSS
FOR LAUGHTER.

GO ON

I MUST CHERISH
AND FIND SAFE HARBOR
FOR THE FIRE
WITHIN ME THAT IS MY
LIFE,

REFLECTION

PAUSE " CATCH YOUR BREATH FOR NOW.

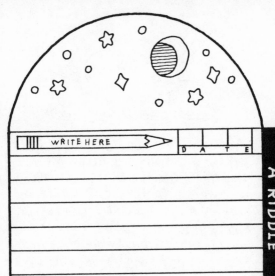

WRITE HERE ➤

D A T E

☆ SWEET BLESSING ☆

MAY YOU SLEEP
WITH PLEASURE
IN A CLOUD OF FEATHERS.

GORDON

ALLOW ME, MY GOD, TO REALIZE THE STRENGTH WITHIN ME, ALLOW ME, MY GOD, TO BE GENTLE TO MYSELF, ALLOW ME, MY GOD, TO HAVE NO REGRETS, TO LIVE MY ALLOTTED SHARE OF LIFE FREELY, AND TO REJOICE IN MY LIFE, LET ME SHOUT TO THE CANYONS IN ME MY SONG OF LIFE" »HOW GOOD IT IS TO BE ALIVE, MY GOD, THANK YOU FOR MY LIFE, «

REFLECTION

PAUSE " KEEP THINGS IN PERSPECTIVE,

| YOUR THOUGHTS | ✏ | D | A | T | E |

☆ SWEET BLESSING ☆

MAY YOU AWAKE
TO FIND STARS IN YOUR HAIR.

A DELIGHT

GO ON

LET ME REMEMBER TO
KEEP MY EYES ON YOUR LIGHT.

LET ME REMEMBER TO
SEEK COMFORT IN YOU,
MY REDEEMER.

LET ME FIND LOVE IN YOU.

REFLECTION

PAUSE " TAKE A WALK AROUND THE BLOCK.

YOUR SPACE

DATE

EUREEKA!

☆ SWEET BLESSING ☆

MAY YOU
SET FIRE TO YOUR
IMAGINATION.

GO ON

DEAR GOD,
I THANK YOU FOR THIS BEAUTIFUL DAY TODAY. I FELT HAPPY AND SO FORTUNATE TO BE ALIVE. I FELT STRENGTHENED BY THE WIND, THE SUN, THE CLEAN AIR. I FELT HEALTHY AND THANK YOU FOR MY GOOD HEALTH. IT IS IMPORTANT TO REMEMBER TO GIVE THANKS AT THESE TIMES.

REFLECTION

PAUSE·· HAVE FUN. COLOR A PICTURE TODAY.

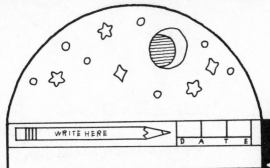

| WRITE HERE | D | A | T | E |

☆ SWEET BLESSING ☆

MAY YOU KEEP YOUR HEART AND MIND OPEN AND FIND A PATH TO HAPPINESS.

GO ON

PRAYERSONG

LEND ME YOUR GRACE, DEAR LORD,
TO WEATHER THIS LIFE MORE
BRAVELY. LEND ME YOUR COURAGE,
MY GOD, TO FORCE AWAY MY
DEMONS. LEND ME YOUR STRENGTH,
MY ROCK, TO BETTER WALK WITH
BOLDNESS.

| REFLECTION |

PAUSE // GIVE YOURSELF A BREAK.

| YOUR THOUGHTS | D | A | T | E |

A MYSTERY

☆ SWEET BLESSING ☆

MAY THE WORDS YOU SPEAK
TURN INTO BIRDS THAT FLY TO THE
HEAVENS.

GORDON

I DON'T WANT TO WASTE MY LIFE WAITING FOR BETTER DAYS AHEAD, WHEN I AM BLIND TO THE BEAUTY, THE RICHNESS AND GOODNESS OF TODAY. OH, LORD, LET ME THANK YOU FOR WHAT I DO HAVE.

REFLECTION

PAUSE " LET YOURSELF BE.

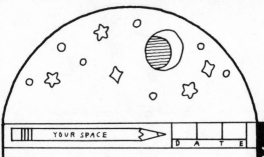

| YOUR SPACE | | D | A | T | E |

☆ SWEET BLESSING ☆

MAY YOU ALWAYS BE ABLE TO
LOOK YOURSELF IN THE EYE
AND LAUGH AT YOUR FOLLIES.

Go BON

OH,
BEAUTIFUL GOD,
ADORE ME THE WAY
I ADORE
YOU.

| REFLECTION |

| REFLECTION |

PAUSE, SMILE, AND DON'T SLOUCH OVER.

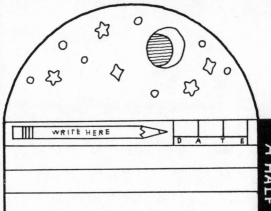

| WRITE HERE | ➤ | | D | A | T | E |

☆ SWEET BLESSING ☆

MAY YOU USE
YOUR NEW DAY TO SING AND PLAY.

GO ON

THERE IS A BRAZILIAN SAYING"
>> EACH DAY YOU MUST KILL A LION. <<

EACH DAY, THEN, WE MUST SLAY THE
FEAR WHICH THREATENS US WHEN
WE AWAKE.

PRAYER IS MY SPEAR.

REFLECTION

PAUSE " GO FORTH.

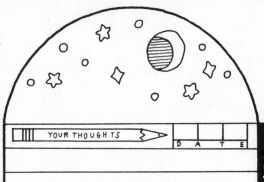

| IIII | YOUR THOUGHTS ⇒ | | D | A | T | E |

☆ SWEET BLESSING ☆

MAY YOU FIND THE WILL
AND STRENGTH
TO SLAY THE DRAGONS WHICH
FRIGHTEN YOU.

GO SON

OH, MY LORD,
LET ME BE BRAVE THIS YEAR. LET
ME SEE THE DAYS FILLED WITH
BEAUTIFUL COLORS AND FLYING
BIRDS. I WILL MARCH AS PROUDLY
AS I CAN IN THE DAYS AHEAD. BUT,
PLEASE, MY GOD, RUN WITH ME, SO
I WILL STUMBLE LESS.
AMEN.

REFLECTION

PAUSE " LISTEN TO THE HUM OF YOUR HEART.

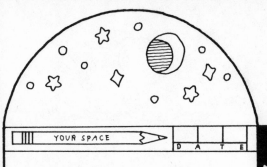

YOUR SPACE	D	A	T	E

☆ SWEET BLESSING ☆

MAY YOU DISCOVER
WONDERFUL TREASURES
THAT ARE NOW HIDDEN FROM
YOU.

GO ON

I SEEK REFUGE
IN YOU, OH LORD, TO
COMFORT ME WHEN I AM
AFRAID, TO LOVE ME WHEN I
FEEL ALONE.

WHEN WILL I LEARN TO BE A REFUGE
TO MYSELF?

REFLECTION

PAUSE·· THINK OF WHAT MAKES YOU HAPPY.

WRITE HERE

D A T E

☆ SWEET BLESSING ☆

MAY YOU BELIEVE
FULLY IN YOURSELF.

GO ON

PRAISE TO YOU, OH LORD,
FOR COMING TO ME IN THE EARLY
UMBRELLA OF DAWN,
YOUR PRESENCE BLOWING AWAY THE
ASHES OF THE DARK NIGHT.
LONG LIVE THIS DAY, LEAVING HOPE
AND FULFILLMENT IN ITS WAKE.

THANK YOU FOR THE LIGHT.

REFLECTION

PAUSE·· BELIEVE IN THE ETERNALNESS OF HOPE.

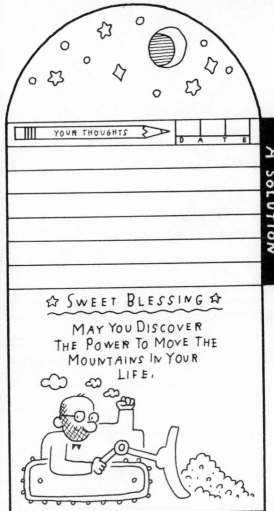

YOUR THOUGHTS | D | A | T | E

☆ SWEET BLESSING ☆

MAY YOU DISCOVER
THE POWER TO MOVE THE
MOUNTAINS IN YOUR
LIFE.

GO ON

HELP ME, LORD,
TO KEEP THE BALANCE IN MY
LIFE.
BY THAT, I MEAN PLEASE HELP ME
FROM SLIPPING INTO DESPAIR
AND LOSING SIGHT OF THE JOYS
AND ACCOMPLISHMENTS
IN MY LIFE.

REFLECTION

PAUSE " FLEE YOUR REGRETS.

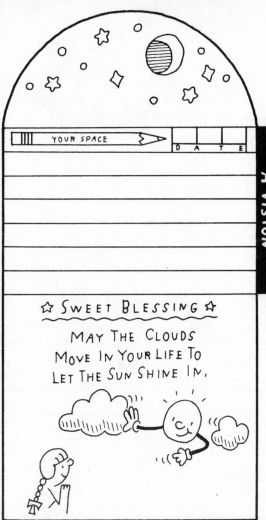

YOUR SPACE

DATE

A VISION

☆ SWEET BLESSING ☆

MAY THE CLOUDS
MOVE IN YOUR LIFE TO
LET THE SUN SHINE IN.

Gordon

YOUR THANKSGIVING

REFLECTION
REFLECTION

PAUSE

WRITE HERE

DATE

YOUR WISH

☆ YOUR SWEET BLESSING ☆

GO ON

DEAR LORD " PLEASE BLESS MY DAUGHTER.
I LOVE HER SO MUCH, AND PRAY THAT YOU
WILL WATCH OVER HER. SHE'S YOUNG AND
IMPETUOUS, AND FEISTY, AND SHE WILL NEED
MUCH LOVE IN HER LIFE.

PLEASE LET HER BLOOM INTO A WONDERFUL
PERSON WHO CAN ENJOY LIFE'S RICHNESS.
SHE IS THE BEST IN ME, LORD, AND IF YOU
LOVE ME A LITTLE, THEN PLEASE ALSO LOVE
MY LITTLE GIRL.

REFLECTION

PAUSE " SHARE SOMETHING WITH SOMEONE.

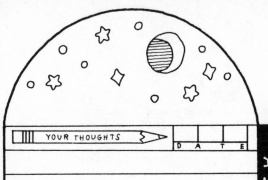

▮▮▮ YOUR THOUGHTS ▸	D	A	T	E

☆ SWEET BLESSING ☆

MAY YOU TOUCH
AND CHERISH
THE CHILD WITHIN YOU.

GO ON

To You I Ask, God, Let Me Have Courage To Ride The Waves That Come In My Life, And To Help Me Renounce My Deep Fear Of Uncertainty. I Know I Cannot Know Everything, And That It Takes A Lifetime To Achieve Some Understanding. But Along The Way, God, Please Give Me Strength To Take Life's Adventures, And To Overcome My Hesitations.

REFLECTION

Pause.. There's Sweet Music To Hear In Life.

YOUR SPACE | D A T E

AN ADVENTURE

☆ SWEET BLESSING ☆

MAY YOU LIVE
TO WALK ON MARS.

MARS

I TALK TO YOU
IN THIS EARLY MORNING HOUR, GOD,
TO COME TO TERMS WITH THE
NIGHT AND TO GATHER STRENGTH FOR
MY NEW DAY. PLEASE STAY
WITH ME FOR I AM AFRAID IN MY
LONELINESS.
OR, ARE YOU ALWAYS THERE
IF I CALL UPON YOU?

REFLECTION

PAUSE " YOU WILL SURVIVE.

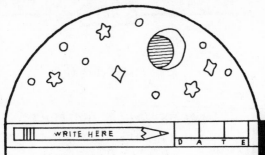

| WRITE HERE | D | A | T | E |

☆ SWEET BLESSING ☆

MAY YOU FIND A SWEET VOICE
WITH WHICH TO SING.

GO ON

JOY

CLOUDS OF JOY

THERE ARE CLOUDS THAT MOVE
   THROUGH THE NIGHT.
THEY LIGHT THE DARKNESS IN
   OUR HEARTS.
THEY ALLOW US TO LOOK WITHIN
   TO SEE THE SWEET CHILD THERE.
THESE CLOUDS OF JOY LET US SHOW
   MERCY TO OURSELVES.

WHEN I THINK OF CLOUDS OF JOY
I SEE PEOPLE RIDING CLOUDS
   AND ENJOYING THE BEAUTY
   OF THE HEAVENS.
BUT MOSTLY, THE CLOUDS OF JOY
   ARE WITHIN US.
THEY ARE THE WINDOWS OF OUR
   SOULS.

JOY

IN THIS
CLOUD
OF JOY

I SEE THE
SUN PEEK
OUT TO
LIGHT MY
WAY.

THIS CLOUD OF JOY

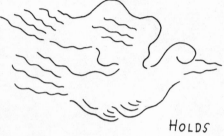

HOLDS
FOR
ME

A BIRD THAT
FLIES SO
GRACEFULLY

DESPITE THE
WIND THAT
BLOWS SO
FORCEFULLY,

IN THIS
CLOUD OF JOY
I DISCOVER
THE PLEASURE OF
SHARING.

JOY

THIS CLOUD OF JOY
HOLDS FOR ME

A LIFE
COMPANION.

HOW ARE CLOUDS OF JOY CREATED?
DO THEY COME FROM ABOVE?
WILL THEY SPILL FROM THE SKY
AND SHOWER US WITH LOVE?
OR DO YOU SEND THEM UP FROM
WITHIN?
ARE THEY OUR THOUGHTS AS THEY
RISE TOWARD HEAVEN?
OUR HEARTSONGS? OUR HOPES? OR
OUR ASPIRATIONS?
CAN THEY BE OUR HUZZAHS?
I WILL SEARCH FOR THE JOY THAT
IS WITHIN ME.

WHAT IS YOUR CLOUD OF JOY?
WRITE HERE

I OFFER THANKSGIVING
TO YOU FOR THE SUPREME
WONDERFULNESS OF LIFE.
THESE ARE THE MOMENTS
OF HAPPINESS I MUST
SAVE TO FALL BACK ON IN
DIFFICULT TIMES.

REFLECTION

PAUSE " PLANT A NARCISSUS IN WINTER.

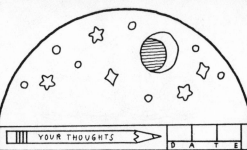

| IIII YOUR THOUGHTS ➤ | D | A | T | E |

☆ SWEET BLESSING ☆

MAY YOU FIND PEACE
AT THE CORE OF YOUR SOUL.

WINTERWISH

GO BON

DEAR GOD,
HOW DO YOU KEEP THE TIGERS OF DOUBT AT BAY? HOW DO YOU KEEP THE BEASTS OF FEAR FROM GNAWING AT YOUR HEART? HOW CAN ONE LIVE A GOOD LIFE IN THIS HARD, CRUEL WORLD? HOW DO YOU BECOME STRONGER? I'M NOT SURE OF THE ANSWERS TO THESE QUESTIONS. ALL I KNOW IS TO PERSIST AND CARRY ON.

REFLECTION

PAUSE " LOOK OUTSIDE YOURSELF.

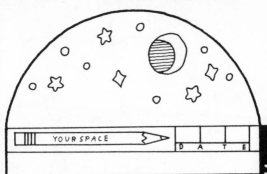

| YOUR SPACE | | | D | A | T | E |

A SADNESS

☆ SWEET BLESSING ☆

MAY YOU FIND SOMEONE TO CLING TO IN JOY AND COMFORT.

GO ON

A BLESSING

OH, LORD,
LET ME LOVE FREELY AND NOT
HOLD BACK,
LET ME FIND THE JOY THAT LIES IN
MY HEART ... LET ME FEEL THE
MUSIC OF MY SOUL,
LET ME FEEL THE BEAUTY AROUND AND
WITHIN ME AND IN THE PEOPLE I LOVE,

REFLECTION

PAUSE ... BE GENTLE WITH YOURSELF.

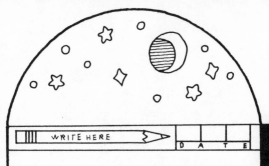

IIII WRITE HERE ⟩	D	A	T	E

☆ SWEET BLESSING ☆

MAY DEEP THOUGHTS COME
TO YOU AND YOU BE GRATEFUL
ENOUGH TO CRADLE THEM.

GO
ON

I AM WORKING HARD THIS MORNING
TO FIND COMFORT IN MY LIFE. I AM
GRATEFUL WITH ALL THE FIRE IN MY
BEING TO HAVE KNOWN WHAT IT IS TO
BE A FATHER AND HUSBAND.
DESPITE THE MANY FALSE STARTS, THE
MANY MISTAKES, I HAVE TRULY DONE
MY BEST, DEAR LORD, AND MY FAMILY
PROVIDES THE ROCK OF MY LIFE.

REFLECTION

PAUSE...LEARN TO LAUGH A LITTLE AT YOURSELF.

YOUR THOUGHTS

D A T E

IDEALS

☆ SWEET BLESSING ☆

MAY YOU BE BLESSED WITH WORK YOU CAN TAKE PRIDE IN AND WHICH CAPTURES YOUR IMAGINATION.

GO ON

DEAR GOD,

I PRAY TO YOU AND REACH
OUT TO THE HOLINESS
WITHIN ME.
I REALIZE THAT I LACK MUCH
POWER. BUT I KNOW, TOO,
THAT I HAVE A SMALL VOICE THAT I
CAN MAKE LOUDER.

REFLECTION

PAUSE... THANK YOUR LUCKY STARS FOR TODAY.

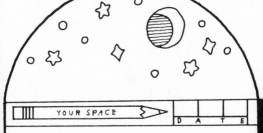

IIII	YOUR SPACE ⮕		D	A	T	E

DREAMS

☆ SWEET BLESSING ☆

MAY YOU MEET THREE ANGELS IN
YOUR LIFE AND KNOW ENOUGH
TO WELCOME THEM.

GO ON

WHY I PRAY

IN TRYING TO COMMUNE
WITH YOU, I BUILD A FORTRESS
TO FEND OFF MY PAIN. I BUILD A
BRIDGE TO MY HEART WHICH
HAS BEEN STARVED FOR
WORD FROM ME.

REFLECTION

PAUSE " DON'T TAKE YOURSELF SO SERIOUSLY.

| | WRITE HERE ⟶ | | D | A | T | E |

A MADNESS

☆ SWEET BLESSING ☆

MAY YOU SURPRISE
EVERYONE " EVEN YOURSELF!

GO ON

I HAVE SPENT
MY WHOLE LIFE
FIGHTING AS BEST I CAN,
AND I HOPE
TO LEAVE THIS WONDERFUL
LIFE
FIGHTING FIERCELY.

REFLECTION

PAUSE·· LOOK FOR A RAINBOW.

| ▓▓▓ YOUR THOUGHTS ▷ | D | A | T | E |

☆ SWEET BLESSING ☆

MAY YOU DISCOVER
THE BELL OF HOPE THAT RINGS
WITHIN YOU.

GO ON

I THANK YOU
FOR SUSTAINING ME,
THE SENSE OF YOUR
PRESENCE
HELPS ME
THROUGH MY DAYS.

REFLECTION

PAUSE·· LISTEN FOR THE OCEAN IN A SEA SHELL.

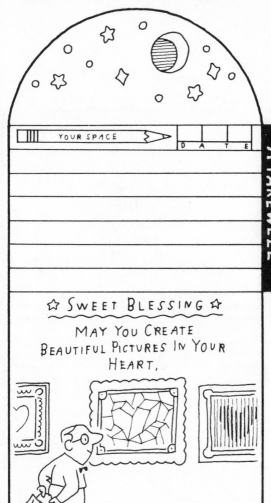

YOUR SPACE ⟹

D A T E

☆ SWEET BLESSING ☆

MAY YOU CREATE
BEAUTIFUL PICTURES IN YOUR
HEART.

HOPE IS THERE,
I KNOW,
BURIED WITHIN THE CREASES OF
MY FEARS.
IT IS WAITING TO
EMERGE,
GIVEN HALF A CHANCE.

REFLECTION

PAUSE·· HOLD ON, WHATEVER YOU DO, HOLD ON.

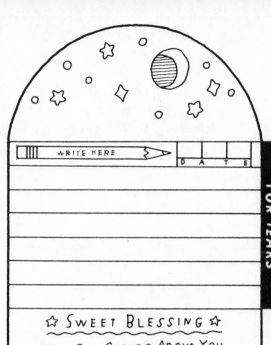

| | WRITE HERE ▷ | D | A | T | E |

FOR TEARS

☆ SWEET BLESSING ☆

MAY THE CLOUDS ABOVE YOU
RAIN DOWN GENTLE FLOWER PETALS.

GoSon

GOD, I AM SO GLAD YOU ARE THERE. TO BE ABLE TO THINK OF YOU GIVES ME SOME CALM, SOME PEACE, SOME STRENGTH. HOW LONELY I WAS WHEN I STOPPED TRYING TO REACH OUT TO YOU.

REFLECTION

PAUSE " DON'T GIVE UP.

YOUR THOUGHTS

DATE

ASPIRATIONS

☆ SWEET BLESSING ☆

MAY YOU FIND
THE BEAUTY WITHIN YOU.

GO ON

WILL...

... MY DAUGHTER REMEMBER ME WITH LOVE
WHEN I AM DEAD AND NO LONGER HERE,
OF THIS WORLD?

... SHE GLANCE UP FROM HER THOUGHTS,
HER WORK, HER SORROWS OF THE DAY TO
REMEMBER ME?

... SHE THINK OF ME WITH LOVE IN HER HEART?

... MY THOUGHTS AND VIEWS STILL INFORM HER?

... SHE TELL HER CHILDREN ALL ABOUT ME?

... SHE BE STRONG IN MY ABSENCE?

REFLECTION

PAUSE ·· WRITE A LETTER TO SOMEONE YOU LOVE.

YOUR SPACE

DATE

HALLELUJAH

☆ SWEET BLESSING ☆

MAY YOU SEE THE SUN RISE
MANY, MANY MORNINGS.

M	Tu	W	TH
14	15	16	17

GO ON

OH, GOD,
GRANT ME THE STRENGTH
TO LIVE MY LIFE,
WHICH I LOVE SO MUCH,
BETTER,
LET ME BE MORE THAN I AM
NOW,

REFLECTION

PAUSE... DO NOT IGNORE YOUR INNER STRENGTHS.

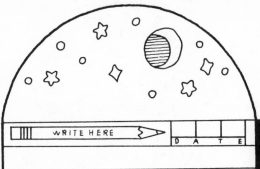

| WRITE HERE ➤ | | D | A | T | E |

☆ SWEET BLESSING ☆

MAY YOU ATTAIN
YOUR HEART'S DEEPEST DESIRE.

A HURRAH!

GO ON

HOW DO YOU BECOME STRONGER AND WISER? IS THERE A MAGIC KEY, OR IS IT THAT YOU BUILD KNOWLEDGE THE SAME WAY A PEARL GROWS, AS LAYER UPON LAYER OF LIFE FORMS AROUND A KERNEL OF TRUTH AND STRENGTH?

BLESS ME, OH LORD.

REFLECTION

PAUSE · MAKE YOUR MAGIC HAPPEN.

| | YOUR THOUGHTS | | D | A | T | E |

☆ SWEET BLESSING ☆

MAY YOUR CRIES
AND WHISPERS BE HEARD.

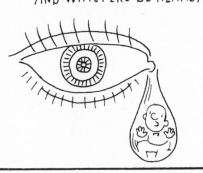

GO ON

LET ME FIND THE TIGER WITHIN.
LET ME BE FIERCE AND CLING TO
   MY LIFE WITH PASSION AND SONG.
MY GOD, LET ME FIGHT TO MY END,
AND LET MY WILL BE STRONG.
LET ME SING WITH FIRM VOICE THE
   SONG OF MY LIFE.
LET ME CLING TO MY SONG AS I DIE,
                              AMEN.

REFLECTION

PAUSE·· YOU WILL FIND STRENGTH· BE PATIENT.

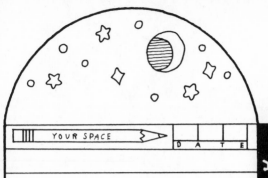

YOUR SPACE		D	A	T	E

☆ SWEET BLESSING ☆

MAY YOU BE BLESSED
WITH GOOD HEALTH, DREAMS TO SPUR
YOU ON, AND, THE UNSELFISHNESS
TO LOVE OTHERS.

A MEMORY

GO ON

MOVING CLOUDS

How Do I Find The
Sun?
That Is The Question…
How Do I Find The
Sunshine In Me?

REFLECTION

PAUSE…LISTEN TO THE LEAVES RUSTLE.

WRITE HERE ➤

D A T E

☆ SWEET BLESSING ☆

MAY YOU FIND
THE MAGIC IN YOU.

GO ON

I SEARCH FOR YOU IN THE AIRY
ABODE OF MY IMAGINATION,
LET ME MEET WITH YOU, MY GOD,
FOR I NEED YOU,
LET ME ADORE YOU, AND YOU WILL
BLESS ME.
I NEED YOUR BLESSING ON THIS
COLD, LONELY DAY.

REFLECTION

PAUSE "SAY" I BELIEVE SUNSHINE HEALS. «

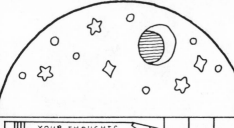

| IIII YOUR THOUGHTS ➤ | | | D | A | T | E |

ACCOMPLISHMENT

☆ SWEET BLESSING ☆

MAY YOU LET YOURSELF
FLY AND SOAR.

GO JON

YOUR PRAYER

REFLECTION

REFLECTION

PAUSE

YOUR SPACE

D A T E

☆ YOUR SWEET BLESSING ☆

GO ON

BLESS ME WITH PEACE OF MIND,
MY GOD. LET ME COME TO MYSELF
AND REJOICE IN MYSELF. LET ME
TAKE PLEASURE IN MY LIFE AND
REMEMBER TO LOVE MY SHORT TIME
HERE. LET ME SLOUGH OFF WHAT
IS UNIMPORTANT AND REJOICE IN
WHAT IS GOOD AND BEAUTIFUL.

REFLECTION

PAUSE·· HAVE A GLASS OF PINK LEMONADE.

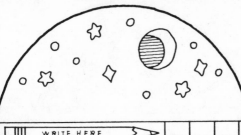

| WRITE HERE ▷ | | D | A | T | E |

SUMMERWISH

☆ SWEET BLESSING ☆

MAY YOU FIND THE PERSON YOU
LOVED AND LOST.

GO ON

» NEVER BE TIMID, «

I TELL MY HEART AND SOUL,

» DO NOT DEPART QUIETLY. «

	REFLECTION	
	REFLECTION	

PAUSE·· REMEMBER THAT YOU'RE STILL ALIVE.

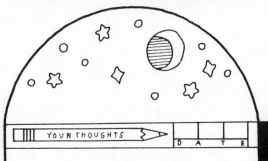

YOUR THOUGHTS	DATE

☆ SWEET BLESSING ☆

MAY YOU LEARN TO SPEAK TO
ANIMALS IN THEIR LANGUAGE.

THIS IS A GOOD TIME, MY LORD. I THANK
YOU FOR ALL YOU HAVE GIVEN ME. I
FEEL TRULY FORTUNATE, AND BLESSED.
I FEEL HUMBLE IN YOUR MERCY AND
GOODNESS TO ME. I THANK YOU FOR
MY BLESSED LIFE. MAY YOU BE THAT
KIND TO ALL PEOPLE.
I WILL TRY TO LEAD A GOOD LIFE FOR YOU.
AMEN.

REFLECTION

PAUSE.. GIVE THE GIFT OF A KISS, OR A SMILE.

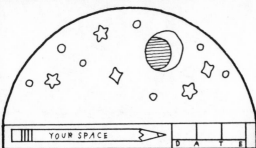

| ▥ | YOUR SPACE | ⟩ | D | A | T | E |

☆ SWEET BLESSING ☆

MAY YOUR HEART ALWAYS SKIP A BEAT
OR TWO WHEN YOU DISCOVER SOMETHING NEW.

GO ON

LET ME RECALL, OH LORD,
IN MY MOMENTS OF FEAR THE STRENGTH
YOU GIVE TO ME WHEN I PRAY TO YOU.
AT THOSE TIMES LET ME REMEMBER,
TOO, THE STRENGTH THAT I HAVE
LET GROW WITHIN ME TO
PERSIST,
AND TO PRESS FORWARD.

REFLECTION

PAUSE·· LOOK FOR PEACE, AND IT WILL FIND YOU.

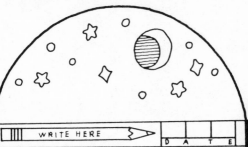

| WRITE HERE | D | A | T | E |

☆ SWEET BLESSING ☆

MAY YOU REMEMBER
THE GOOD TIMES IN YOUR LIFE
AND CROWD OUT THE BAD MEMORIES.

A BELIEF

I AM THANKFUL, MY GOD,
TO BE ABLE TO GATHER WITH
MY FAMILY
AND EXPERIENCE THE RICHNESS
OF OUR LIVES TOGETHER.
ALLOW ME TO HAVE MANY MORE
YEARS OF LIFE WITH THEM.

REFLECTION

PAUSE·· THERE IS STILL MUCH MUSIC IN YOUR LIFE.

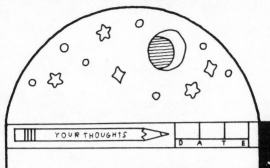

| | YOUR THOUGHTS | | D | A | T | E |

☆ SWEET BLESSING ☆

MAY YOU NEVER
LACK FOR FRIENDS.

GORDON

PSALM

LET THERE BE PEACE IN OUR
HEARTS, CALM IN OUR SOULS
AND LOVE IN OUR BEINGS.
LET US CONSIDER THE TRULY
IMPORTANT AND KEEP FAITH
WITH THE SIGNIFICANT.
LET US NOT FORGET TO LOVE ONE
ANOTHER AND SEEK OUR JOY,
WE MUST MAKE THE EFFORT TO LIVE BETTER.

REFLECTION

PAUSE " BE CREATIVE WITH A MEAL.

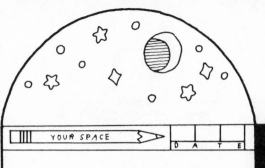

A POEM

| IIII | YOUR SPACE ➤ | D | A | T | E |

☆ SWEET BLESSING ☆

MAY YOU DANCE AND PRANCE
AND SCALE TALL BUILDINGS IN
ONE LEAP.

GO ON

DEAR GOD,
LET WAR STOP. LET THE
DEVASTATION BE NO MORE.
LET THE WORLD BE SAFE AND
    THE MADNESS AMONG US CEASE.
WHEN THE BOMBS EXPLODE, MY LORD,
MY HEART BREAKS. WHO WILL PICK
UP THE PIECES OF MY FELLOW BEINGS?

REFLECTION

PAUSE " CATCH THE SUNLIGHT IN YOUR HANDS.

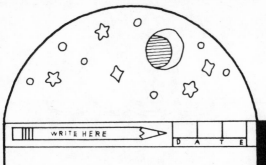

WRITE HERE ✏ →	D	A	T	E

A LOVE

☆ SWEET BLESSING ☆

MAY YOUR CRIES TURN TO
LAUGHTER
AND YOUR SIGHS TO JOY.

GO JON

THANK YOU
FOR THE
JOY
OF THIS
BEAUTIFUL
DAY.

REFLECTION

PAUSE·· THERE IS A WILD HEART IN EACH OF US.

YOUR THOUGHTS

DATE

An Understanding

☆ SWEET BLESSING ☆

MAY YOU NEVER LOSE
YOUR FUNNY GIGGLES.

SOME BASICS

AM I HEALTHY?
DO I HAVE A ROOF
  OVER MY HEAD?
ARE THE PEOPLE
  I LOVE SAFE?
DO I HAVE A LOVING
  FAMILY?

REFLECTION

PAUSE·· FIX YOUR FACE AND SMILE.

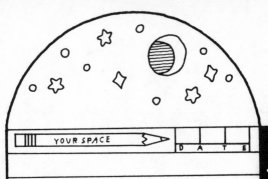

|  YOUR SPACE | D | A | T | E |

☆ SWEET BLESSING ☆

MAY YOU LEARN
TO FLY.

GO ON

WHEN I WRITE TO YOU,
DEAR GOD,
I THINK I AM ALSO TALKING
TO MYSELF,
TRYING TO CALM ME AND HELP
EASE ME ALONG.

REFLECTION

PAUSE··SHOW SOMEONE HOW TO SMILE.

WRITE HERE →

DATE

☆ SWEET BLESSING ☆

MAY YOU REALIZE
THE FULLNESS OF
YOUR BRAVE NATURE.

GO ON

As a Child I Would Lie In My Bed At Night And Pray So Fervently To A Powerful God In Heaven To, Please, Help Me And Keep My Family Together. Let Me Be Safe, Let Not Any Harm Come To My Mother And Father, I Prayed. I Believed So Strongly Then, God. Can I Believe That Way Again? Can I Find Refuge In You Once More?

REFLECTION

PAUSE...LAUGH NOW, AS YOU NEVER DID BEFORE.

YOUR THOUGHTS

DATE

AutumnWish

☆ SWEET BLESSING ☆

MAY YOU DANCE TO THE MUSIC
OF WHISPERING BUTTERFLIES,

DEAR GOD OF MINE,

I MUST HAVE FAITH IN MY FUTURE. I MUST BELIEVE IN MYSELF AND IN MY ABILITY TO GROW AND SURVIVE. IF I CAN'T BELIEVE IN MYSELF, GOD, THEN ALL IS LOST, FOR NO ONE CAN GIVE ME WHAT I CANNOT GIVE MYSELF.

REFLECTION

PAUSE.. SLOW DOWN. STAND FAST. SIT STILL.

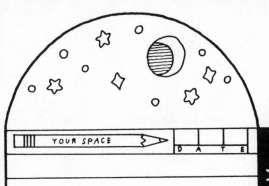

| | YOUR SPACE ▷ | | D | A | T | E |

☆ SWEET BLESSING ☆

MAY YOU LEARN TO
GIVE TO OTHERS.

GO SON

ALLOW ME TO SURMOUNT
MYSELF,
I PRAY THAT YOUR LOVE FOR ME,
OH LORD,
WILL BLEND WITH MINE FOR YOU,
SO THAT I MAY BECOME
STRONGER.

REFLECTION

PAUSE··PUT UP THE »GONE FISHING« SIGN SOMETIMES.

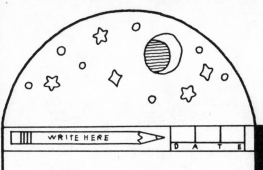

| | WRITE HERE | | D | A | T | E |

☆ SWEET BLESSING ☆

MAY YOU BECOME
THE RUBY·RED PERSON
YOU ALWAYS WANTED TO BE.

GO BON

DEAR GOD,
I THINK OF YOU A LOT,
AND I FEEL LESS LONELY
IN THE WORLD.
I FEEL YOU ACCOMPANY ME
WHEREVER I GO.
THANK YOU.

REFLECTION
REFLECTION

PAUSE... PAY ATTENTION TO YOUR HEART.

MAY YOU FIND THE CLOUDS OF JOY WITHIN YOU.

BILL ZIMMERMAN, the creator of *The Little Book of Joy*, has been a questioner all his life. A journalist for more than twenty years and a prize-winning editor, Zimmerman is special projects editor for *Newsday*, one of the nation's largest newspapers. His other books are *How to Tape Instant Oral Biographies*, a book that teaches you how to capture your family stories on audio and video tape; *Make Beliefs*, a magical gift book for the imagination; *Lifelines: A Book of Hope*, which offers comforting thoughts; and *A Book of Questions to Keep Thoughts and Feelings*, a new form of diary/journal.

TOM BLOOM is driven by his dreams, and they often appear as drawings for *The New York Times, The New Yorker, Newsday, Fortune, Barron's, Games,* and others. His hopes and joys include his family and friends as well as this planet on which he spends most of his time.